The Teachi[ng]

425 Dha[mmapada]

IN ENGLISH POETRY

*'Essential for wise is to focus his mind,
And not allow attachments of any kind.
Such detachments will cleanse his mind,
And Nirvana he shall, here only find.'*

DHAMMAPADA (6/88)

Translated by
Dr. Sant Kumar Bhatnagar

HINDOOLOGY
BOOKS

Published by

HINDOOLOGY
BOOKS

An Imprint of
Pustak Mahal®, Delhi

J-3/16 , Daryaganj, New Delhi-110002
☎ 23276539, 23272783, 23272784 • *Fax:* 011-23260518
E-mail: info@pustakmahal.com • *Website:* www.pustakmahal.com

London Office
51, Severn Crescents, Slough, Berkshire, SL 38 UU, England
E-mail: pustakmahaluk@pustakmahal.com

Sales Centre
10-B, Netaji Subhash Marg, Daryaganj, New Delhi-110002
☎ 23268292, 23268293, 23279900 • *Fax:* 011-23280567

Branch Offices
Bangalore: ☎ 22234025
E-mail: pmblr@sancharnet.in • pustak@sancharnet.in
Mumbai: ☎ 22010941
E-mail: rapidex@bom5.vsnl.net.in
Patna: ☎ 3294193 • *Telefax:* 0612-2302719
E-mail: rapidexptn@rediffmail.com
Hyderabad: *Telefax:* 040-24737290
E-mail: pustakmahalhyd@yahoo.co.in

© Copyright : Author
ISBN 978-81-223-1023-8
Edition : May 2008

Printed at : Param Offsetters, Okhla, New Delhi-110020

<u>**Dedication**</u>

This book is dedicated to:
My revered parents, who provided
good values to me and whose blessings
continue to inspire me.
My spouse Indira, my daughter Deepti,
and my son Tarun who have been the
guiding force behind this book.

———————

CONTENTS

✧※✧

PREFACE

Although there are volumes of teachings of Siddhartha Gautama, later called Buddha, these are considered to be canonical. The Lord Buddha – the incarnation of Lord Vishnu, gave sermons at Benaras (now called Varanasi, situated in Uttar Pradesh in India) called *Dhamma-chakka-ppavattana-sutra* (The Turning of the Wheel of *Dharma*). The text of these sermons was extracted from the stories of the life of Gautama Buddha which form the Holy Book called **Dhammapada** (in Sanskrit called *Dharampath* i.e. the Path of *Dharma*). It contains 423 sayings categorised into 26 chapters based on different attributes of man. Sayings of Lord Buddha show the path to salvation and must be followed with utter sincerity and devotion and practiced in principal in daily life so that one can be absolved of the process of rebirth.

The sayings are narrated in very simple methods giving appropriate similes to make them easily understandable. These sayings are not supposed to be static and unchanging, but are paths for us to practice.

Lord Buddha explained some of the aspects which need a careful heed if one needs to get rid of pain and anguish. According to him, man suffers from infinite pain and suffering from the cycle of rebirth i.e. after death he again comes back into this world (*Samsara*). He returns into this mortal world based on his old actions and has to pay the price in every rebirth for his old births' actions. The process of rebirth is, therefore, a very painful experience.

According to Lord Buddha, renunciation or asceticism is not the answer to get out of these sufferings. One has to work hard to attain *nirvana*, salvation or liberation from the cycle of rebirth. To attain *nirvana* one needs to meditate, letting go all the lustful desires, anger and pride. That way man would be able to absolve himself from the rut of the cycle of birth and death. The man who is close to attain *nirvana*, is called the Awakened One i.e. '*Buddha*'. He does not have to come back into this mortal world again and he is freed from the cycle of life and death.

Although *Dhammapada* has been translated from Pali language into English language by many dedicated worshippers of Buddha's teachings, I have tried in my own humble way, to place before you this book in the form of rhyming poetry.

My attempt is not to undermine or seek recognition over others who have translated *Dhammapada* in English language. They have done an excellent work. It is only that when I started reading the scripture lately I decided to present it in poetic form.

I hope that this book will be unique, as reading poetic script is more pleasing and joyful. I shall be happy to receive views and criticism from my readers so that the book could be improved in the next edition.

I would like to record my thanks to my elder brother, Professor Uttam Chand, who has been the most inspiring force and who made useful corrections and gave suggestions to improve the script. The other source of immense help has been Mr. S.K.Roy and his editorial staff at Pustak Mahal who gave very useful suggestions to bring the book to its present form.

—**Dr. Sant Kumar Bhatnagar**
Bangkok, Thailand

LORD BUDDHA

According to Hindu Philosophy, Lord Vishnu descends on this planet to reinstall *Dhamma* (Sanskrit - *Dharma*) and guide the people in the direction of virtue, law and nobility. Lord Buddha, God himself, was the ninth reincarnation of Lord Vishnu. However, Thais, the people of Thailand, believe him to be the incarnation of Lord Brahma – the creator of this universe.

Buddha is the one who is fully enlightened or awakened and has overcome desires, cravings, aversion, delusion and ignorance and is completely liberated from suffering.

These are the *trividha-dwara* (the three doors) of Buddhism:

- *Thought*
- *Word*
- *Deed*

It was in 563 BC, a son was born to Queen Mahamaya and King Shudhodan, the ruler of a small kingdom on the Indo-Nepal Border. Mahamaya gave birth to this divine child while she was on her way to her parent's house. Soon after the birth, she died in a week's time leaving the child in the care of the second queen. The child was named Siddhartha Gautama.

The royal astrologers predicted that this child will either be a great monarch or a great saint relinquishing the entire worldly luxuries of a monarch. King Shudhodan decided to provide the prince with all the luxuries of life in the palace so that he did not have to witness hardships of life. The prince was educated at home by the revered teachers. The king further decided to marry him at a very young age so that he could be involved in worldly affairs and keep him away from possibility of converting to sainthood. At the age of sixteen, he was married to Yashodhara, a beautiful princess from a neighbouring state. Within a couple of years of their marriage, Yashodhara gave birth to a male child who was named Rahul.

However, destiny prevailed and once, when Siddhartha was being driven to places of interest, a change in his heart became noticeable. The king had given clear instruction to charioteer to follow a particular route but prince persuaded the charioteer to change the route. Along the way he noticed — a sick man; an old man; and a dead person being carried in a funeral procession. This was start of change in his mind and he decided to renounce the princely life and luxuries.

In search for truth, he roamed from place to place, meeting all types of men, saints, seers, sages. No body could wash off his mental debacle and the questions in his mind remained unanswered. He decided then to undertake severe penance along with his five friends. Undergoing physical hardships transformed him into an emaciated skeleton. He became so frail, lean and starved that he fainted when a girl from a nearby farm offered him rice porridge and milk. This offended his five friends who left his company. It was then that Siddhartha realised that fasting and penance were not the solution.

When he became well, he started meditation under the *peepal* tree (holy tree of Hindus). On the 49th day, he experienced the divine light and was enlightened. Thus at the age of 35, Siddhartha was an enlightened one and he was called Gautama Buddha.

He started preaching his enlightened views in Pali. His language and style of teaching was very simple which could be understood by all. These preachings became the *Sutras* and are recorded in *Dhammapada* in Pali language.

BASIC CONCEPTS OF LIFE AS VIEWED BY BUDDHA

The four truths given below have been preached by Lord Buddha to his disciples as they are beneficial and are fundamental to holy life. They lead to dispassion, disenchantment and cessation of suffering and ultimately to the blessed state of happiness *(nirvana)*.

Although there are volumes of literature available on his teachings which run into over 80,000 articles, they can be summarised as under:

1. Four Noble Truths
2. Eightfold Path
3. Five Percepts

Four Noble Truths of Lord Buddha

1. The Truth of Suffering *(Dukha)*

Lord Buddha discovered that no one can escape suffering in one's life. Life's suffering can be either physical or mental. Physical sufferings are mostly due to age which leave a man suffering with aches and pain, loss of speech, hearing and sight and difficulty in eating food. The disease strikes all young and old and can result in great pain and anguish and eventually cause death which brings grief. This suffering has to be borne alone, which is far worse. Similarly mental agony and pain due to loneliness, frustration, depression, despair and anger also has to be endured. All men who are born have to die ultimately.

2. The Truth of the Cause of Suffering *(Samudaya)*

The second truth is that suffering is caused by craving and wishful desires and greed to attain name and fame, wealth and all worldly possessions. These eventually give rise to anger, greed, fear and finally to utter despondency and pain. Therefore, one needs to control one's desires and cravings to rid of suffering. Sickness and old age come to all men in life.

3. The Truth of the End of Suffering *(Nirodha)*

The third truth is to overcome suffering to achieve rapture, happiness and contentment. This can possibly be attained by eschewing wishful desires and cravings. This eventually leads to *nirvana*. Death is inevitable for all.

4. The Truth of Eightfold Path leading to the End of Suffering *(Magga Marga)*

The fourth truth is eightfold path enunciated by Lord Buddha to end these sufferings. Renunciation is the way to attain peace and happiness.

The Eightfold Path

The eightfold path enunciates the way to end suffering leading to *nirvana* or *moksha* or in attaining salvation from the cycle of rebirth. Lord Buddha delivered his first sermon on *dharma* in the Deer Park at Sarnath in Varanasi in India. This was called *'The Wheel of Dhamma'*. Every man is able to recognise sooner or later that suffering which enters our life brings pain and anguish to us due to our craving for fulfillment of desires. When a person realises this, then the person is said to have attained the right view of life. Eightfold path can be categorised into main three subheads as given below:

Three Qualities	Eightfold Path
Wisdom *(panna)*	Right Understanding
	Right Thought
Morality *(sila)*	Right Speech
	Right Action
	Right Livelihood
Meditation *(samadhi)*	Right Effort
	Right Mindfulness
	Right Concentration

These are briefly described below:

1. Right Understanding

We must understand that the change is a fact of life. One must not stick to one's longings. We must understand life as it is. We must understand that happiness comes from within and not from outside. All things are transient in this world. This kind of right understanding would enlighten us so that we may not crave for happiness.

2. Right Thought

Seeds of suffering take root in our mind. We must not allow ideas to take root which breed desires and cause suffering and pain. We should be able to recognise between the right and wrong thoughts. Ideas which cause suffering are fifteen defilements, preached in Buddhism. These are:

Greed, ill-will, hostility, denigration, dominance, envy, jealousy, hypocrisy, fraud, obstinacy, presumption, conceit, arrogance, vanity and negligence.

Lord Buddha realised that these defilements of mind can be done away by six means:

- **Restraining** ideas which poison the mind.
- **Using** all resources to cultivate peace of mind.
- **Tolerating** all misfortunes and not to surrender to wrong thoughts.
- **Avoiding** all that spoils the mind. Tend ideas which nurture and purify the mind.
- **Destroying** all the defilements from their roots forever.
- **Developing** all skills only towards achieving peace and serenity of mind.

3. Right Speech

We all speak and that is the normal behaviour of a man. However we must weigh our words before we utter them. Words, once spoken, can not be retrieved. A person is generally judged by his speech and it is advisable to be reticent in speech. Bad words can be worse than a dagger and wounds they leave can be far more dangerous and painful. Lord Buddha described four ways of speech which can bring peace to our lives and to those surrounding us.

- **Honest words** help us to achieve peace as these are based on truth. Hence the speech should be factual.

- **Kind words** never ever harm anyone, rather generate an atmosphere congenial to peace and happiness.

- **Nurturing words** give comfort and do not bring pain and grief and neither harm anyone. Thus they bring lasting peace to everyone.

- **Worthy words** should be carefully chosen so that they are appropriate for the purpose. They should be soothing and sweet to the ears. They should be free from ulterior motives like gossip, untruth, selfishness etc. and speech should not be abusive.

4. Right Action

All our actions have to be right actions. Sometimes it is difficult to choose what is right and what is wrong. And our judgment gets clouded by defilements of the mind. Our action has to be such that it brings peace and happiness to others. Right actions do not change often. Hence we should delve deep into our heart and mind and decide the right action. This is possible if we respect life, earn all that we have and control our desires rather than they control us, which will be catastrophic.

5. Right Livelihood

In this life we have an opportunity to liberate ourselves and also help others to get rid of sufferings and find peace. So we must follow the way of life which breeds peace all around and does not create impediments. One should not indulge in trades such as, trading in arms and intoxicants, drugs, prostitution, trading of humans and unscrupulous means to acquire wealth, which directly or indirectly harm other living beings or systems.

6. Right Effort

We remain quite absorbed in our own life and pleasures which we seem to have gained with great efforts. It is not easy to let them go. A very resolute mind is required to do away with the so-called dearly attained things in order to follow the path of liberation. Our effort has to be firm like that of a drowning man trying to struggle for breath. One must have goodwill towards all other living beings, and uphold their dignity. It can be achieved by making some efforts:

- To make an effort to prevent unwholesome what has not come.
- To make an effort to destroy unwholesome that has come.

- To make an effort to produce the wholesome that has not yet come.

- To make an effort to cultivate the wholesome that has come.

7. Right Mindfulness

If we control our mind, we can overcome sufferings. Lord Buddha preached four methods to be mindful and to unlock secrets that are able to exercise influence on our lives:

- **Body** must be taken care of for its well-being. We can focus our breath, movements, our actions and body parts to achieve serenity and equanimity.

- **Feelings** can be internal and external. Their vicissitudes need to be observed to break our fondness to clinging.

- **Mind** is another component which needs to be mastered. Our thought process has to be monitored in a way that we remain calm and serene.

- **Mental qualities** govern our behaviour. We need to govern these qualities rather than they dominate us. We must overcome desires, lethargy, anxiety and dubiousness. We must develop qualities which can peep into our heart and mind so that we can discriminate between good and bad actions and follow only the good actions.

8. Right Concentration

Mind is very turbulent and wanders all around like a rudderless ship without any means and purpose. If it is allowed to roam around the way it likes, one becomes slave to desires which breed fear, anger and greed leading to utter ruination. It is necessary to master the mind and control it so that it does not flutter around. This is possible by indulging in meditation which is nothing but concentration of mind. Regular meditatve exercises will keep the mind under control and bring peace and joy, breath by breath. It shall also be able to help abandon pain and pleasure which are the main causes of unhappiness.

Five Precepts

The five precepts form the basic code of ethics for a Buddhist. They were followed by Lord Buddha and are followed by his followers in the *Theravada* (Thai) and *Mahayana* traditions. These precepts are:

- Refraining from taking life by killing of living beings.
- Refraining from stealing i.e. taking what is not offered.
- Refraining from sexual misconduct like adultery, rape, exploitation etc.
- Refraining from false speech which amounts to lying.
- Refraining from intoxicants of any kind which lead to heedlessness.

Significant Features of Dhammapada

When Lord Buddha passed away, almost 500 of his *Arhant* and disciples, led by Monk Kashyapa, gathered at Rajagaha. They decided to write down the salient features of preaching of Lord Buddha during the past many years, so that they can be the moral and spiritual guide to many of the present monks or to those who will be there in future. With the *guru* no longer with them, they took up the massive job and faithfully jotted down the salient features of over 300 discourses of the Buddha. In final form, it was placed in written scribe in *Pali* language which was called Dhammapada.

Dhammapada has since then been translated into many languages. It is the most beloved scripture of Buddhists. The salient features of the teachings of Lord Buddha enshrined in this book, preach not only to the monks but the entire mankind at large, the path of *dhamma*. The path of *dhamma* is no doubt very tedious and full of impediments, but it is necessary and is binding on us all to tread on *dhamma* so that we could be useful human beings. If there is no *dhamma*, the whole world will be ruled by rogues and there will be no respect to each other. Only path of *dhamma* has saved this mankind from ruination.

Bouquet of Wisdom

The very first chapter of Dhammapada says that our thoughts govern us and we tend to do right or wrong by virtue of these thoughts. However, in the ensuing chapters he explains that we can master and control our mind so that bad thoughts do not dare come near us and we think right and act right. These are also two of the eightfold truths enunciated by Lord Buddha and explained in early pages.

Dhammapada embraces all the four truths, eightfold path and five precepts, and shows the way to ameliorate oneself by abandoning desires, carnal lust, greed and wishful thinking. All these things give rise to fear, anger and greed which are the main cause of man's ruination. It becomes more apparent, therefore, that man should behave well with his kind speech, his kind words, and be reticent in useless gossips. Man should remain calm and serene to be happy and this is only possible if he masters his senses and keeps them under his control:

> *Our thoughts only, direct our actions,*
> *Noble speech provide us delectations.*
> *With mind in peace, happiness follows,*
> *And never leave us like our shadows.*

[1/2]

Human mind is unsteady and wanders faster than wind. It falls prey to evil elements faster as they provide quick benefits. It becomes necessary to control the mind fully so that it does not sway here and there. Once the mind is tamed it will work as per our will:

Mind is fickle, shaky and unsteady,
To wander aimlessly, it's always ready.
If one can justly practice forbearance,
One receives joy and delight in abundance.

[3/35]

Lord Buddha exhorts people to follow an example of scented flower which spreads its fragrance all around. Likewise, a wise person spreads his wisdom in all directions irrespective of the direction of the wind:

Be it sandalwood or flower of any kind,
Its fragrance never flows against the wind.
But wisdom of wise disperses all over,
Pierces through wind, every place it covers.

[4/54]

Lord Buddha further advises that we should always remain vigilant and agile. We should never allow lethargy and laziness to take over our lives or while away our useful time in sleep and indolence. Fools and ignorant carve their own path towards ruination because of ill-deeds and sinful actions. But wise are free of desires and are indifferent to heat and cold, and pain and pleasure. They are thus respected everywhere:

Wise never allow negligence to breed,
Nor do they permit any sensual greed.
They always remain immersed in meditation,
And are recipient of abundant delectation.

[2/27]

Lord Buddha also touches upon the evil part of man, the old age which leads to suffering and punishment to ignorant and violent people. Evil must be eradicated from the roots or else it comes back with vengeance and overpowers the mind:

> *Behold this beautiful diseased body of man,*
> *Which is a mass of sores of creative brain.*
> *Body joined by limbs, of many pattern,*
> *And is neither permanent nor certain.*
>
> [11/147]

Lord Buddha tells us to get out of ignorance and illumine the world like the moon which comes out of clouds and brightens the world. Thus one can get enormous happiness and rapture. To achieve the Eternal Bliss, one needs to become Buddha and attain enlightenment:

> *When an evil man leaves bad conduct,*
> *Starts pursuing and doing good act.*
> *Like moon he becomes a man good and proud,*
> *That lightens the world, coming out of cloud.*
>
> [13/173]

Attachment to family and things is the main cause of desire and greed. One who is detached to these elements, is free from fear and close to happiness:

> *Grief arises from pleasure,*
> *And from pleasure comes fear.*
> *One who is free from pleasure,*
> *Is free from grief and fear.*
>
> [16/212]

Lord Buddha also states the eightfold path which leads to *nirvana* and how one can get rid of impurities. Eightfold path has already been discussed in earlier pages. Lord Buddha advises people to do noble deeds during this birth as the journey of a man from birth till death is very painful and full of troubles. We all are the victims of our bad deeds in the earlier birth and have to undergo the journey again and again. This journey is not very comfortable and one remains tangled in this cycle of rebirth and suffering. Hence it is advisable to follow virtuous path and not to cling to the attachments and desires so that one can attain *nirvan*a, deliverance from the cycle of rebirth:

> *Of paths, best is the eightfold,*
> *Best of truths is the fourfold.*
> *Virtuous is, who is detached and free,*
> *He is best of the men who has eyes to see.*
>
> [20/273]

Finally there is a mention of monks, the holy men, who are called *Brahmin*s. They have to possess certain characteristics to qualify as holy men. Saffron clothes or matted long hair do not make a man Monk or *Brahmin*, unless he possesses certain virtues explained in the last chapters. If they do not follow the required tenets, they are destined to dwell in hell in their next birth:

Many persons who wear yellow dress,
Purity of mind they do not possess.
Such wrong-doers end up in hell,
In the next birth, in hell they dwell.

[22/307]

Thus the gist of the preachings is to indulge in good deeds to wash off the sins of earlier birth and shed off attachments and desires to attain *nirvana*, the deliverance from the cycle of rebirth.

Dhammapada does touch upon all the Fourfold Truths and the Eightfold Path which are full of immense spiritual knowledge on *dharma* which we should devoutly follow.

CHAPTER - 1

THE PAIRS
(*Yamakavagga*)

This chapter narrates the dualities and how they influence the person. The dualities are like good-bad, heat-cold, happy-sad, truth-lie etc. Lord Buddha dwells upon how man's thinking can influence him in all respects. It is the thought process of a man which makes him do right or wrong things and finally end up in happiness or sadness as the case may be. He exhorts people to cleanse up their thoughts so that they could be balance-minded.

> *Thoughts get recorded in our mind,*
> *Then invite us to deeds of evil kind.*
> *Pain and agony they continue to impart,*
> *As foot of an ox follows the moving cart.*
>
> [1/1]

> *Our thoughts only, direct our actions,*
> *Noble speech provides us delectations.*
> *With mind in peace, happiness follows,*
> *And never leaves us like our shadows.*
>
> [1/2]

> *Some mean persons kick and beat,*
> *They claim mastery over defeat.*
> *Some indulge in robbery and arson,*
> *Hatred becomes their vile passion.*
>
> [1/3]

But some are of different nature,
Hatred in their hearts they never harbour.
They neither beat anyone nor pilfer,
Nor pride themselves as the winners.

[1/4]

Hatred never ever kills hate,
Hatred-only love can annihilate.
It is well within Yogi's knowledge,
This age-old rule, we must acknowledge.

[1/5]

Evil-minded persons fail to know,
That they, who quarrel, perish and go.
Self-controlled wise know the fact well,
Hatred never they allow to dwell,

[1/6]

Persons who are not serene and calm,
Eat unhealthy foods even if these harm.
They are destroyed by temper and lust,
Like weak tree uprooted in a thrust.

[1/7]

But persons who possess equanimity,
Who eat food, nutritious and healthy.
They are not ruined by anger and lust,
Like rock is not shaken by the tempest.

[1/8]

Persons who want to wear saffron attire,
But have not cleansed mind of sins-entire.
Composure and equanimity, they do not possess,
Are not worthy of wearing the saffron dress.

[1/9]

Persons who are endowed with balance,
And embrace truth and temperance.
Such persons are worthy of all praise,
Qualify to wear saffron clothes with grace.

[1/10]

Those persons who fail to discriminate,
Basics of truth-untruth, they can not state.
Doomed are they to utter confusion,
Untruth to be truth, if they imagine.

[1/11]

He who understands the basics of truth,
And also contrast of truth and untruth.
As paradigm of truth, is never lost in life,
Virtuous truth remains in him forever rife.

[1/12]

Roof of poorly-thatched house is weak,
And is torn apart when torrential rains leak.
Likewise passion invades timid, weak minds,
Importance of meditation, it then reminds.

[1/13]

Roof of well-thatched is not weak,
Rain water there can not ever leak.
Passions fail to subjugate strong mind,
When wise are freed of desires of all kind.

[1/14]

Persons who indulge in ignoble deed,
Lament and repent if once they heed.
Then such deed brings grief and dolour,
In the present world and the other.

[1/15]

If persons indulge in noble deed,
And perceive the purity of their deed.
They relish and enjoy abundant rapture,
In the present world and thereafter.

[1/16]

Persons who indulge in sinful deed,
And become cognizant of such misdeed.
They suffer incessant agony in both the worlds,
And their sufferings multiply manifolds.

[1/17]

Happy is the one who is virtuous and wise,
With every virtue, delights tend to rise.
His happiness then knows no bounds,
In both the worlds, his joy compounds.

[1/18]

A person may recite Holy Scriptures,
But never acts upon what he preaches.
He is unable to enjoy holy life, anyhow,
And is like cowherd, counting others' cows.

[1/19]

A Person though recites few scriptures,
But he does practice what he preaches.
Being free of passion, illusion and greed,
Is verily holy; finds joy within his reach.

[1/20]

CHAPTER - 2

EARNESTNESS
(Appamadavagga)

This chapter deals with earnestness or watchfulness. Lord Buddha explains how a watchful man can work his way up and reach *nirvana* by controlling his sense organs. Contrary to that, a careless person is insolent, sloth, lazy and useless and spends his entire time in sleep, sensuality, greed and false pride. Such a person never ever achieves *nirvana* and comes back to this mortal world.

> *Vigilance is the path to immortality,*
> *Negligence leads to path of mortality.*
> *Vigilant person never ever dies,*
> *Careless faces perdition, never survives.*
>
> [2/21]

> *Stature of vigilant continues to grow,*
> *And his virtues too tend to glow.*
> *Noble knowledge then continues to greet,*
> *At every step, pleasure touches his feet.*
>
> [2/22]

> *Wise, who have perception of vigilance,*
> *And who meditate with perseverance.*
> *They enjoy the knowledge of nobleman,*
> *And delights of Supreme Bliss, they attain.*
>
> [2/23]

Person who is resolute and of clear mind,
Is calm, possessing equanimity of mind.
Self-restrained and follows noble doctrine,
His glories continue to grow with discipline.

[2/24]

Those who keep senses under command,
And remain ever watchful and on their guard.
They always make their own noble niche,
Which no storm can ever flinch.

[2/25]

Ignorant is debased and careless fool,
Considers vanity his treasured tool.
Vigilance is the best jewel of the noble,
Who hates self-love and is kind and liberal.

[2/26]

Wise never allow negligence to breed,
Nor do they.permit any sensual greed.
They always remain immersed in meditation,
And are recipient of abundant delectation.

[2/27]

Vigilant wise is never lax and slack,
And ascends to wisdom of higher track.
He is like a man at the top of the mount,
Gazing at sad-unwise in the valley down.

[2/28]

Lethargic sleeps away the useful moments,
Remains slow in speed, passive and unwell.
Wise remains awake and alert indeed,
Leaves everyone behind like a swift steed.

[2/29]

By virtue of being an attentive lot,
Meghavan rose to the Lordship of gods.
Vigilant are always valued and praised,
Negligent are condemned and debased.
(Meghavan – God of Rain)

[2/30]

Monk who delights in earnestness,
And who gauges danger of carelessness.
He moves around like a forest fire,
And all fetters he can set afire.

[2/31]

Monk who takes pleasure in vigilance,
And fears not the negligence.
From higher glory, he never does decline,
And rightful nirvana, he is likely to find.
(Nirvana-salvation)

[2/32]

CHAPTER – 3

THE MIND
(Cittavagga)

Mind is very turbulent and restless. It runs here and there at its own will.. It is very important that one controls his mind totally so that it listens to him rather than man listens to the mind. Once the mind is under control, sensuality, greed, pride can not overpower it and such a man thus achieves equanimity and is capable of attaining *nirvana*.

Fletcher aligns and straightens the shaft,
When he crafts a precise and best dart.
Wise man controls and conquers his mind,
That is restless and turbulent like wind.

[3/33]

The fish writhes, twists and turns around,
When thrown out of water, on the ground.
So does the mind flutter and quiver,
And try to free it from noble cover.

[3/34]

Mind is fickle, shaky and unsteady,
To wander aimlessly, it's always ready.
If one can justly practice forbearance,
One receives joy and delight in abundance.

[3/35]

Mind is subtle and is difficult to shelter,
At will, it always runs helter-skelter.
Wise men do guard and control their mind,
Which fetches them delights of all kind.

[3/36]

Mind is a lone wanderer and is elusive,
Though in every heart it does live.
When mind is kept under subjugation,
From evil thoughts it gains liberation.

[3/37]

But person whose mind is not under control,
And faith in scriptures who never does hold.
Confusion in such misplaced person, remains,
And peace of mind he never ever attains.

[3/38]

Person whose mind is free of carnal desire,
Which is not fazed by dishonour or admire.
And hatred who never ever endear,
That awakened person is free of fear.

[3/39]

This body is fragile like an earthen pot,
Its mind must be defended like a fort.
Wise slay Mara with the sword of wisdom,
And never let attachments nearby come.
(Mara- evil thoughts)

[3/40]

Alas! Before long, this body will die,
And upon this earthly ground, it will lie.
It will cast aside feelings senile,
Like a charred log, it becomes futile.

[3/41]

When thoughts are wrongly directed,
Extensive hurt is then afflicted.
Very difficult is to endure that damage,
Than that is given by enemy's hateful image.

[3/42]

When thoughts are correctly directed,
Greater happiness is then surely meted.
They then deliver far greater pleasure,
More than what parents and relatives offer.

[3/43]

CHAPTER - 4

THE FLOWER
(Pupphavagga)

Man can be compared to a flower. Like a flower, man takes birth and eventually dies. Some flowers emanate fragrance all around while some are devoid of such quality. Man should train himself akin to fragrant flower, so that he can spread the fragrance of knowledge all over. Fragrance of flower is short-lived and is little. However, the fragrance of knowledge is permanent and can disperse even against the flow of fiercest wind.

Who shall master this earth?
Who shall master gods, and death?
And virtues on the path who shall gather,
Like connoisseur, who sorts the precise flower.

[4/44]

Disciplined follower can certainly overcome,
Yama's domain and of gods' kingdom.
The sage chooses the path of virtues ever,
Like an expert gardener picks up right flower.
(Yama-God of Death)

[4/45]

The body is mortal and eventually perishes,
Akin to mirage like froth, the body vanishes.
One must snap bonds of flower-smeared dart,
And overpower the death — Lord Yama's path.

[4/46]

Hedonist who indulges in sensual thirst,
Evil and wicked death, puts him to rest.
Like the village ravaged, when in slumber,
By the fearful storm displaying its temper.

[4/47]

Hedonist, who is besotted with lust,
Finds that nothing can quench such thirst.
He longs to seek only carnal pleasures,
And is carried away by the evil desires.

[4/48]

Bee never hurts and injures the flower,
Nor does destroy its fragrance and colour.
Hops and collects nectar from flowers,
So does wander village to village, sage follower.

[4/49]

Man should not criticise other person,
Nor see acts of omission and commission.
He should judge what he has done or not,
And peep into inner-self to gauge his fault.

[4/50]

They are like flowers which are colourful,
Who speak words, flowery and beautiful.
But if they never practice what they tell,
They are like flowers devoid of scented smell.

[4/51]

Flowers are beautiful and elegant to behold,
Stock of immense fragrance they unfold.
Wise men are like flowers with scented smell,
Because they practice,   noble words they tell.

[4/52]

When flowers are lying anywhere in a pile,
One can make garlands of variegated style.
Mortal man is subject to cycles of rebirth,
Ought to perform virtuous deeds with mirth.

[4/53]

Be it sandalwood or flower of any kind,
Its fragrance never flows against the time.
But wisdom of wise disperses all over,
Pierces through wind, every place it covers.

[4/54]

Fragrance which sandalwood emits,
Blue lotus and jasmine also transmit.
Fragrance emitted by virtues is continual,
But that of flowers is limited and temporal.

[4/55]

Sandalwood, jasmine and lotus all,
They radiate fragrance, far too small.
Noble path wise devoutly tread,
Fragrance amongst gods; they spread.

[4/56]

Noble path, evil men never travel,
And hardly know this path so well.
Virtuous are imbued with thoughts noble,
Realise salvation eschewing deeds ignoble.

[4/57]

Roadside trash also produces useful things,
Advisable is not to ignore as it has something.
Here fragrant lotus flowers mostly originate,
Which we call a heap of trash and rubbish waste.

[4/58]

Similarly there appear some wise men,
Among the blinded crowd of ignorant ones.
Like lotus flower someone literate,
Shines among crowded ignorant illiterate.

[4/59]

THE IGNORANT FOOL

(Balavagga)

This chapter explains about a fool or an ignorant. The ignorant fool is unaware of the Supreme Truth and as such is proud, obstinate and debase. He is incapable of reaching the Supreme Truth of life, even if he tries his best. It is the duty of the educated and Yogi to not let him go astray and impart him sufficient knowledge of the Supreme Truth. It is the duty of the ignorant fool to spend some time with such learned people.

To the sleepless, night appears very long
To the weary, ten miles' walk seems long.
Long seems the cycle of death and birth,
For ignorant knows not, path of Eternal Mirth.

[5/60]

Disciple, who finds not a friend in travel,
A friend, who is better or of equal level.
Better for him to continue travel alone,
For it is folly to have a fool as companion.

[5/61]

Fool is misled by his false ego and pride,
Claiming that he has wealth, he has child.
Knows not he; one's self is not one's own,
Why does he then speak of wealth and son.

[5/62]

To that extent, fool is considered wise,
When he admits his folly of being unwise.
But fool who considers himself as wise,
Knows not, he is verily a fool and unwise.

[5/63]

Fool may spend entire life with a wise,
Never does the Truth he conceptualise.
Just as spoon knows not the soup's taste,
Flavour of truth knows not the illiterate.

[5/64]

Learned in a company of an intelligent,
Perceives the Truth in just a moment.
Such an educated one is of higher rung,
Just as flavour of soup, detects tongue.

[5/65]

Ignorants are devoid of sense of wisdom,
Enemy of themselves they finally become.
They perpetrate and commit sinful act,
And bitter fruits they then always collect.

[5/66]

They are ill-advised to perform ill-deeds,
That gives rise to taste not so sweet.
Worst and agonising are their outcome,
Prone to grief and painful they become.

[5/67]

Actions are considered well-done of course,
Which bring good taste and no remorse.
When one performs right and noble deeds,
Permanent joy and rapture one receives.

[5/68]

Ignorant thinks nectar flows from action,
Until and unless its fruits spew poison.
When he realises, fruits are not honey,
His sufferings get laced with agony.

[5/69]

Practice of austerity, ignorant may assume,
And for months Kusha grass, he may consume.
Even one-sixteenth part he fails to achieve,
Which the wise and intelligent men perceive.
(Kusha-type of grass)

[5/70]

Just as the milk takes time to turn sour,
So are the effects of evil deeds, by far.
They follow the fool like fire-smoulder,
Akin to the fire that ashes cover.

[5/71]

Wrong action when known to ignorant,
Receives grief and sorrows - abundant.
His head splits by pain of moral turpitude,
And ruins and destroys all his virtues.

[5/72]

Ignorant always longs for reputation,
Among people, he looks for veneration.
Among mendicant, demands seniority,
And among monks, demands authority.

[5/73]

In every action of fool, pride lurks,
He thinks himself as doer of all works.
Ignorant fool is besotted with pride,
Full of ego, as if lives in fool's paradise.

[5/74]

There are only two paths on this earth,
One for deliverance, other for wealth.
Let Monk detach himself from lust,
And always strive for wisdom; he must.

[5/75]

CHAPTER – 6

THE WISE
(Panditavagga)

Wise men are respectful men and one should keep company with them because they show the real path to *nirvana*. Yogi controls his senses and stays away from greed, pride and ignoble thoughts even though they are close to him. He attains *nirvana* and is absolved of the cycle of birth and death into this mortal domain.

> *One ought to keep company of the wise,*
> *Who praise virtues; faults who criticise.*
> *Such friends unearth his virtue's treasure,*
> *Mitigating woes and generating pleasure.*
>
> [6/76]

> *Let wise instruct, advise, carp and cavil,*
> *To restrain others from committing evil.*
> *From noble person, wise receive delight,*
> *But evil person offers nothing but spite.*
>
> [6/77]

> *Let a man not leave company of the wise,*
> *To keep evil away, only wise can advise.*
> *Let man choose noble man as his friend,*
> *His virtues will then continue to distend.*
>
> [6/78]

Let a man follow virtuous and noble path,
Which provides his mind tranquility fast.
Path of Dhamma, when a man does follow,
Eternal Bliss automatically start to flow.
(Dhamma-truth)

[6/79]

Like irrigator guides the water into fields,
Like the shaft of an arrow, Fletcher builds.
Like a carpenter shapes the wood he grinds,
Wise similarly control and conquer the mind.

[6/80]

Even when stormy winds ferociously blow,
Strike the rock but can not move and throw.
Similarly wise man is not affected at all,
Be it an honor or dishonor, rise or fall.

[6/81]

Deep lake always remains still and quiet,
Its water too is then clear and bright.
Mind of wise man becomes pure and clear,
To teachings of Dhamma if he lends an ear.

[6/82]

Wise never ever talk of lust and desire,
Nor for attachments do they aspire.
They display not, any sorrow or rapture,
Whenever touched by grief or pleasure.

[6/83]

Such a wise is virtuous par excellence,
And always is ready to offer assistance.
He ever remains upright in his wisdom,
Yearns not for wealth, son and kingdom.

[6/84]

Only select few amongst those wise,
Cross-over to shore of other side.
Rest of the people remain stuck on the shore,
Even if they try, find hard to cross over.

[6/85]

Those who receive Dhamma's wisdom,
And leave the Dhamma's path seldom.
They verily face no fear and difficulty,
To cross over the ocean of mortality.

[6/86]

Those who are enriched with intelligence,
And have abandoned all dark ignorance.
And have abdicated home for solitude,
They then enjoy - the eternal beatitude.

[6/87]

Essential for wise is to focus his mind,
And not allow attachments of any kind.
Such detachment will cleanse his mind,
And Nirvana, he shall here only find.

[6/88]

Wise who is immersed in enlightenment,
And has given up desires of entertainment.
Free of evil lusts, righteous he remains,
In this very life, nirvana he attains.

[6/89]

CHAPTER – 7

THE PERFECT ONE
(Arahantavagga)

The Perfect One (The Absolute) is a person who is free of all dualities and is not effected by them. He spends a solitary life in forests, where no sensual objects can reach him. He constantly remains in search of *nirvana* and is calm and pure of mind like ocean where noisy rivers enters but ocean stays calm and pure. He eventually attains *nirvana* and is freed from the fetters of cycle of rebirth for ever.

> *Wise who has completed cycle of rebirth,*
> *Becomes insular to any sorrow or mirth.*
> *And who has gotten rid of attachments,*
> *He verily is liberated by enlightenment.*
>
> [7/90]

> *Swans never cling themselves to one pond,*
> *They hop to this pond, hop to that pond.*
> *Likewise wise man renounces his love for home,*
> *To find solace, from place to place they roam.*
>
> [7/91]

> *Those having no worldly possessions to enjoy,*
> *Take regulated food and have realised void.*
> *Their holy path is far difficult to espy,*
> *Like the path of birds who fly in the sky.*
>
> [7/92]

Those who are indifferent to joy and delight,
Delivered of corruption, unattached to diet.
Their holy path is very difficult to espy,
Like the track of birds who fly in the sky.

[7/93]

Like the trainer who has trained the steed,
Wise trains himself, to control senses indeed.
Having given up ego, false pride and greed,
To admire them, even the gods do cede.

[7/94]

Wise remains tolerant like earth planet,
Like Indra's pillar is upright and honest.
He is transparent like the deep clear lake,
Attains liberation , rebirth needs not take.

[7/95]

They verily are wise , peace who teach,
And are serene and reticent in speech.
Wise who have thus attained deliverance,
Possess equanimity par excellence.

[7/96]

One who has perceived the Almighty God,
And remains indifferent to good and bad.
And who has abandoned all worldly desires,
He verily is a wise man, we must admire.

[7/97]

Be it a forest or be it a small town,
Be it a valley or be it a mount.
Whenever wise man, there resides,
Joy of all the worlds, there abides.

[7/98]

Yogi likes to live in forest of woods,
Where he always feels happy and good.
Forests are delightful places to reside,
From lust and greed, diversion they provide.

[7/99]

CHAPTER - 8

THE THOUSANDS
(Sahassavagga)

This chapter deals with thousands i.e. man may live for thousand years yet he can not achieve *nirvana*. Man must conquer his mind before he could embark upon any venture. His company with Yogi, in reverence, is far batter than his thousand years of life here. There is no simple way to achieve the Supreme Truth.

> *Better to speak useful words, may be few,*
> *Make the mind peaceful, fresh and anew.*
> *If one speaks flowery words with no contents,*
> *They are futile, devoid of peace and content.*
> [8/100]

> *It is no use to speak thousands of verse,*
> *Which are meaningless and are adverse.*
> *Recitation of one useful verse is far better,*
> *Peace and joy all around which can scatter.*
> [8/101]

> *There is no need to recite thousands of verse,*
> *Which are meaningless and are adverse.*
> *Recitation of one verse of Dhamma is better,*
> *Peace and joy all around which can scatter.*
> (Dhamma-dharma or religion)
>
> [8/102]

Thousands and millions perish in the war,
Conqueror claims himself as winning star.
But verily he is the greatest winner,
Who has conquered his mind forever.

[8/103]

Victor in war is necessarily a villain,
Such victory is subject to defeat again.
Victory over self is doubtlessly superior,
Than victory that is achieved over others.

[8/104]

Victor in war is necessarily a villain,
Such victory is subject to defeat again.
Victory over self is better than over others,
Which even Devas, Mara or Brahma can not reverse.
(Devas-the gods, Mara-evil, Brahma-the Creator)

[8/105]

Superior is one-time honour offered to the Seer,
Which provides immense peace and pleasure.
Better than centuries of sacrifices of all time,
Even if made every month a thousand times.

[8/106]

A person may abandon and dwell in forests,
Worship Agni for hundred years without rest.
The serenity attained is nowhere near,
Than won by momentary service of the Seer.
(Agni-God of Fire)

[8/107]

A person makes oblation all through the year,
So that he is absolved of all sins and fear.
Such oblation provides not even quarter of cheer,
Than the service and honour offered to Seer.
[8/108]

There are four principal codes of conduct,
For a respectful man, primary is elder's respect.
It imparts good looks and health to become strong,
Imparts abundant happiness for life to be long.
[8/109]

Only a day's purposeful life is enough to live,
When mind is under control, is meditative.
Here life of hundred years is of no good,
During meditation, mind tends to elude.
[8/110]

A day's life of meditation is enough to live,
When mind is under control and is pensive.
Life of hundred years here is not worthy,
When mind is un-meditative and is filthy.
[8/111]

A day's life of happiness is enough for wise,
When he works hard and incessantly tries.
But person who does not work and is inactive,
His life of hundred years is unworthy to live.
[8/112]

A day's life is far better and sound,
Who can observe the changes all round.
But one who is non-observant and not agile,
Hundred years of life is useless and futile.

[8/113]

Far better is to live for a day with activity,
To know and perceive his own immortality.
But one who fails to discern his immortality,
Hundred years of life runs into futility.

[8/114]

The ultimate truth is the supreme bliss,
And one day's life is enough to know this.
But if one fails to perceive supreme road,
Useless is to live hundred years on this globe.

[8/115]

CHAPTER - 9

THE EVIL
(Papavagga)

Lord Buddha exhorts that all noble deeds must be done quickly without losing any time. Otherwise men get laced with evils which offer faster benefits and are then caught into the web of evils from where it is difficult to get liberation. The results of noble deeds are slow but permanent. Hence noble men get heaven and evil men go to hell.

> *Perform all good deeds with haste,*
> *Cast off evil thoughts, as a total waste.*
> *For a lazy, good work is hard to capture,*
> *Evil seizes him with its tempting rapture.*
>
> [9/116]

> *If a man performs an evil task whatsoever,*
> *He should know, no pleasure he can gather.*
> *Aught to avoid repeating it again and again,*
> *As sum effect of evil will be endless pain.*
>
> [9/117]

> *If a man decides to do righteous deed,*
> *And again and again continues to repeat.*
> *He is the lawful recipient on this earth,*
> *To get abundant glee without any dearth.*
>
> [9/118]

Good deeds fetch happiness and prize,
Till the evil deeds do not start to rise.
If a man conceives of doing evil deeds,
Righteous work ceases and evil succeeds.

[9/119]

Evil deeds fetch pain, anguish and sorrow,
Till the good deeds do not start to grow.
When a man conceives of doing good deeds,
Evil work ceases and nobleness succeeds.

[9/120]

Fools are bereft of the basic wisdom,
That evil once departed never ever come.
Just as drop by drop the pitcher gets filled,
Evil makes inroad inch by inch and gets instilled.

[9/121]

Let us not underestimate nobleness of good,
That it never returns if departs for good.
Like drop by drop water fills the pitcher,
It returns bit by bit, making wise richer.

[9/122]

As merchant travels with wealth and gold,
Carries small escort, avoiding unsafe road.
Similarly a man avoids the path of evil.
Evil that poisons the life, acts like a devil.

[9/123]

Whoever has no wound on his hand,
Can safely carry poison with bare hand.
Poison never poisons hand with no wound,
Evil never harms him who does no wrong.

[9/124]

Whoever hurts and harms an innocent,
Who is righteous pious and benignant.
The evil strikes back with revengeful gush,
Like the sand thrown against the windy gust.

[9/125]

Some people are subject to rebirth,
Wrong-doers go to hell, full of filth.
Go to heaven, who have done good deeds,
Attain nirvana *who have abandoned needs.*

[9/126]

Neither in the sky nor in the ocean,
Nor in the caves, nor in the mountain.
None can escape from the evil deed,
Nor on this earth can hide indeed.

[9/127]

Some people are subject to rebirth,
Evil-doers go to hell, slough of filth.
Go to heaven that always do good,
Attain nirvana *who detaches for good.*

[9/128]

CHAPTER – 10

PUNISHMENT
(Dandavagga)

Man wants to live forever but the fear of death always lurks in his mind. Man wants lots of happiness even at the cost of taking away happiness of other fellow beings. Such a person is punished in ten ways which are very painful and distressing. Hence man should stay away from evil deeds to escape from such punishments.

> *Every person living on this earth,*
> *Fears and shiver from the death.*
> *One should avoid violence in every way,*
> *Should neither slay nor provoke to slay.*
>
> [10/129]

> *Name of death sends quiver to everyone,*
> *Who does not want to live, there is none.*
> *Comparing with others becomes then vital,*
> *And to eschew any path which is fatal.*
>
> [10/130]

> *Anyone who seeks happiness and rapture,*
> *Has no right to rob happiness of others.*
> *If someone by violent means does destroy,*
> *Happiness hereafter, he does not enjoy.*
>
> [10/131]

But one who seeks happiness and rapture,
And tries not to destroy happiness of others.
He is then a recipient of joy on this earth,
And also enjoys happiness even after death.

[10/132]

Do not ever speak words which are curt,
As they give others a very painful hurt.
From angry words, anger emanates,
Which leads one another to retaliate.

[10/133]

Like a broken gong does not vibrate,
One should be serene and not retaliate.
Then he is calm, akin to a broken gong,
And attains nirvana , anger is all gone.

[10/134]

Like a cowherd, the cows who drives,
Using a club , to the pasture he guides.
So do the old age and the death,
Control life of beings on this earth.

[10/135]

When an ignorant commits an evil,
Unable to realise, that fool - so devil.
Victim of stupidity, he is wicked and vile,
And is like the one, singed by fire alive.

[10/136]

A person who uses violence to harm,
Especially those who are not armed.
Aggressive and offensive, if he remains,
One of the following **ten states,** *he attains.*
[10/137]

Cruel sufferings, infirmity and body injury,
Loss of health and mind, and gruesome agony.
Persecution by King, loss of house and wealth,
Loss of relative, *goes to hell after death.*
[10/138-140]

Such a person if fails to overcome desire,
He is deprived of purifying his life entire.
Even if squats, sleeps on the floor, keeps fast,
And stay naked with matted hair, applies ash.
[10/141]

Man who is well-attired, chaste and calm,
And castes away passion, afflicts no harm.
Possesses balanced mind , does good to other,
He is a Sage and Brahmin of the first order.
[10/142]

It is usually rare to find somebody,
Who is verily subdued by modesty.
They avoid reproach and do not blame,
Like horse avoids whip, if duly tamed.
[10/143]

Similar to the horse when touched by whip,
Be strenuous, eager, let faith take the grip.
Meditation helps discern truth in entirety,
And helps generate in a man moral purity.

[10/144]

Like irrigators guide the water into fields,
Like the shaft of an arrow, Fletcher builds.
Like carpenters shape the wood they grind,
Likewise wise control and conquer the mind.

[10/145]

CHAPTER – 11

THE OLD AGE
(Jaravagga)

Old age shows scars of our deeds. This body is ephemeral and eventually dies and merges with the soil. Lord Buddha says, "*Look at this old emaciated body, on which flesh and blood has been plastered. It shows signs of all stresses, strains and distress. Afterwards, the hollow bones akin to a hollow pumpkin spread all around which can not offer happiness to a man, seeing what will happen to him also. But noble deeds of a man stay here forever.*"

> *While this world is ever ablaze,*
> *Why is there jubilation and craze.*
> *Why do we not try to seek the light,*
> *When shrouded in dark twilight.*

[11/146]

> *Behold this beautiful diseased body of man,*
> *Which is a mass of sores of creative brain.*
> *Body joined by limbs, of different pattern,*
> *Which is neither permanent nor certain.*

[11/147]

> *Aging body becomes very weak and frail,*
> *A home for disease and turns fragile.*
> *This (body) heap of corruption disintegrates,*
> *Death becomes the end of life – ultimate.*

[11/148]

When these white dried   bones,
Cast aside like gourds in autumn.
Then how can one derive rapture,
To see such bones strewn all over.

[11/149]

This body is nothing but a type of fortress,
Stack of bones, plastered by blood and flesh.
It is a depository of death and decay,
And repository of deceit and pride's display.

[11/150]

Even the chariots of king wear out by age,
This body also decays owing to old age.
The virtues found by Seers ever remain,
They never age,   Seers do proclaim.

[11/151]

If a man does not try to learn,
He can be compared to an oxen.
As the ox ages, only its flesh grows,
Likewise ignorance of man tends to grow.

[11/152]

To find the creator of life I roamed in vain,
Even I went through births again and again.
Very painful is the experience of rebirth,
To search the creator of life and death.

[11/153]

Having gone through this cycle of rebirth,
To make this house (life) , is not any worth.
Where rafters (bones) are broken, ridges (joints) are torn.
My mind has attained nirvana, desires gone.

[11/154]

People who practice not, the Holier Truth,
And do not acquire wealth during their youth.
Like a withered crane, grow old and languish,
Which perishes in the pond without any fish.

[11/155]

Those who have not lived the holy life,
Acquired not, wealth during youthful life.
Their life is just like a blunt arrow,
He wails later with a sigh of sorrow.

[11/156]

CHAPTER - 12

THE SELF
(Attavagga)

We all like our 'self'. Obviously we must also look after our 'self'. To remain away from evils we must learn to control our minds. Evil can wrap around us and kill us the same way as a creeper can strangle the tree and kill it. Evils give a man slow-death as also noble deeds fetch happiness slowly. Man should eschew sins as he himself has to give account of his sins and accordingly has to come back to this mortal world. In this chapter, Lord Buddha advises that we should act fervently on our bounden duties.

> *If a person holds himself really dear,*
> *He ought to watch himself with care.*
> *The wise ought to keep his agile tight,*
> *At least in one of three watches at night.*
> [12/157]

> *Let a person practice on himself first,*
> *What he wants to teach to the rest.*
> *To guide others, he is then very fit,*
> *As training oneself is indeed difficult.*
> [12/158]

Let a person perceive what is right,
That way he shall not be defiled.
To teach others, he is then fully adept,
As training oneself is indeed difficult.

[12/159]

Only 'self' is the protector of 'self',
Who else could be master, nobody else.
When a person has controlled his mind,
He gains mastery which is hard to find.

[12/160]

Evil done by a man, is his own creation,
Born in himself, it is the real causation.
Evil destroys them who are unwise and vicious,
Like diamond breaks the stone precious.

[12/161]

Man who is very corrupt and immoral,
He is then brought down to a level.
Where one's enemy would like him to be,
Like the creeper that strangles the Sal tree.

[12/162]

Evil actions are easy to perform,
Which fetch no gain but only harm.
But it is difficult to do good work,
Where kind and beneficial effects lurk.

[12/163]

Fools scorn at the religious scripture,
And scorn at them, so holy and pure.
They eat 'Katha' fruit for destruction,
And are at last condemned to perdition.
(Katha –poisonous fruit)

[12/164]

One does wrong oneself and suffers,
One does good oneself, becomes purer.
No one can purify somebody else,
Purity and impurity depend on 'self'.

[12/165]

One's own duty, one ought not neglect,
Even though duty of others be perfect.
Let one understand his own welfare,
And should tread on this path with care.

[12/166]

CHAPTER – 13

THE WORLD
(Lokavagga)

This chapter deals with the world. Lord Buddha advises to get out of ignorance and embrace the bright light of wisdom. As the moon lightens the entire world once it comes out of dark clouds, so should man brighten this world with his wisdom once he overcomes his ignorance. We should follow the scriptures and duties enumerated in religion and show our reverence to them.

Do not support false ordinance,
And do not indulge in negligence.
Do not accept any wrong notion,
Attach not to any mundane passion.

[13/167]

Wake up and be upright in rectitude,
Observe and practice good attitude.
One who pursues the kind manners,
He then lives happily now and thereafter.

[13/168]

Practice the canons of holy precepts,
And do not pursue immoral conducts.
In Eternal Bliss , the virtue rests,
Both in this world and in the next.

[13/169]

When a person does acknowledge,
This world is a bubble and a mirage.
And that this world of ours to be as such,
Then even King of death can not search.

[13/170]

This world — come and look at it,
It looks like painted royal chariot.
The foolish are immersed in it,
While the wise are unattached to it.

[14/171]

When the moon sneaks out of the cloud,
Its silvery light illumines the world around.
Likewise careless becomes wise,
When care they begin to exercise.

[13/172]

When an evil man leaves bad conduct,
Starts pursuing and doing good act.
He is like the moon and feels very proud,
That lightens the world when out of cloud.

[13/173]

The world is dark and is also blind,
Only a few can see through and find.
As birds escape from the netted screen,
Only a few are able to go to heaven.

[13/174]

Swans fly and traverse the path of the sun,
Men go through air by their psychic acumen.
Wise who have conquered evil and its host,
Absolved of rebirth, reach heaven's post.

[13/175]

One who has transgressed the law,
And who has once flouted the law.
Such a person scorns at another world,
There is every chance, repeat he would.

[13/176]

Misers never go to the gods' kingdom,
And fools do not ever praise freedom.
The wise men in giving, enjoy pleasure,
And are blessed with joy thereafter.

[13/177]

Better is reward of reaching the stream,
Than sovereignty over this earth supreme.
Than the path to go to heaven of gods,
Than the Lordship over three worlds.

[13/178]

CHAPTER – 14

THE ENLIGHTENED ONE
(Buddhavagga)

A person who has achieved enlightenment and complete wisdom is called Buddha. No body can show him the path to Supreme Truth, rather people should look to him for directions. A person gets this birth in human form after going through many painful births and should try that he does not have to come back and go through such a painful and dismal journey again. Only a select few achieve this feat.

One, whose victory can not be beaten,
And whose victory can not be undone.
Then what direction can Buddha be given,
Who is trackless, infinite and awakened.

[14/179]

By what path can you lead Buddha – the infinite,
Who has no passion for worldly lust and delight.
Buddha who has no entrapping and embroiling,
And has no path and is free from craving.

[14/180]

The wise ones are devoted to meditation,
And they delight in the quiet renunciation.
They are like Buddha, awakened and aware,
Even gods envy them and hold them dear.

[14/181]

It is very difficult to be born as man,
So is life of mortal, hard to discern.
Difficult is, hearing of the Sublime Truth,
And hard is, achieving the Buddhahood.

[14/182]

What does Buddha teach?
And what does he preach?
Abstain from evil and practice good,
That would purify the mind for good.

[14/183]

One who strikes others, is not a hermit,
One who insults others, is not an ascetic.
Enduring patience and restraint is austerity,
And thus nirvana is the Supreme Eternity.

[14/184]

Not to strike and not to blame,
Remain calm and aught to restrain.
Moderate in eating , solitude in living,
Awakened one, spreads these teachings.

[14/185]

Lust is less pleasure and more agony,
No one can buy content, even with money.
Lust is devil; its life is of short span,
It has short taste but causes immense pain.

[14/186]

Wise keeps distance from lust mundane,
And finds himself free of grief and pain.
Even heavenly pleasures offer no repose,
To get rid of desires is his sole purpose.

[14/187]

When fear overpowers a person,
Helter-skelter then he does run.
Driven by fear he looks for refuge,
Goes to shrines, hills, forests and groves.

[14/188]

This is not safe and that is not safe refuge,
He finds running around is not of any use.
None of the above is the safe sanctuary,
And thus there is no deliverance from misery.

[14/189]

When Dhamma tenets are followed religiously,
And one remains committed to community.
And refuge is taken with the Supreme,
Four Noble Truth are perceived by him.

[14/190]

Once Four-fold truths are perceived by a person,
He understands cause of suffering and its origin.
He also realises then the way to end suffering,
As to how Eightfold path can eliminate suffering.

[14/191]

The refuge with the Supreme is ultimate,
As all sufferings, this refuge does mitigate.
The man is relieved of all pain and suffering,
And thus finds happiness more fulfilling.

[14/192]

It is not easy to find a man of wisdom,
He is not born everywhere in every home.
But wherever such a Seer takes birth,
The family thrives and enjoys mirth.

[14/193]

Happy is the birth of Buddha,
Happy is the teaching of Dhamma.
Happy is Sangha, the community's union,
Happy is the peace seeker's devotion.
(Buddha-the awakened one; Dhamma-truth; Sangha-community)

[14/194]

One who pays homage to awakened one,
As also respects the disciples of awakened one.
For they have shed off the evil desire,
He then also deserves everyone's' admire.

[14/195]

Person giving reverence to those deserving,
May they be awakened or follower being.
They are then rid off grief and sorrow all,
And their merit can not be fathomed at all.

[14/196]

CHAPTER - 15

HAPPINESS
(Sukhavagga)

Lord Buddha says that *nirvana* is the only path to Supreme Bliss. Man has to work hard and he should try to inculcate good deeds wherever he resides amongst people. This will then show him the path to *nirvana*, deliverance from the cycle of birth and death.

Happily indeed we live with smiles,
Remain friendly amongst the hostiles.
Amidst hostile men, we dwell,
Free of hatred, over others we excel.

[15/197]

Indeed we live with smile happily,
Amidst the afflicted, live cordially.
Amongst afflicted men, we dwell,
And free of affliction, we swell.

[15/198]

Let us live in joy free from lust,
Live among lustful, without lust.
Amidst the passionate, we dwell,
Free of cravings, we must dwell.

[15/199]

Let us live in joy, free from greed,
Live among the greedy, without greed.
Possessing nothing, with joy let us live,
And like the gods, feed ourselves on bliss.

[15/200]

Victory breeds only hatred and disgust,
Defeat breeds misery and distress.
One who is indifferent to either,
Lives in peace and joy forever.

[15/201]

There is no fire equal to lust,
And no crime equal to disgust.
There is no pain akin to body like this,
Higher than peace, there is no bliss.

[15/202]

Hunger or carving is the greatest illness,
And so is disharmony, the supreme illness.
Whoever truly knows and realises this,
Knows that nirvana is the greatest bliss.

[15/203]

Man's supreme possession is health,
And contentment is the supreme wealth.
Best is the relationship of friendly trust,
Nirvana is Eternal Joy – the highest thrust.

[15/204]

Whoever enjoys the taste of solitude,
And the taste of peace and its beatitude.
He is then absolved of evil and grief,
And enjoys the taste of Spiritual Bliss.

[15/205]

It is sweet to meet with the Seer,
To live with him is a greater pleasure.
But association with fools fetches no gain,
And lead one to slough of grief and pain.

[15/206]

Being with fool is like being with foe,
Where the grief and pain tend to grow.
But being with wise, new joy does begin,
As is realised while meeting kith and kin.

[15/207]

If you meet a man, who is wise and noble,
And is learned, enduring and responsible.
Better keep company of such luminary star,
As the Moon follows the path of fellow stars.

[15/208]

CHAPTER - 16

AFFECTION
(Piyavagga)

Love and affection is another cause of pain and anguish. Departure from the loved ones leaves pangs of anguish and fear. Lord Buddha advises that one should shed off mundane attachments and even attachments to loved ones. Only a detached person is capable of entering into the world of *nirvana*.

> *Whosoever gives oneself to distraction,*
> *And does not care for meditation.*
> *Follows sensual desires, abandon holy quest,*
> *Finally envies the one who meditates best.*
>
> [16/209]

> *Let none cling to what is dear,*
> *And not cling to what is not dear.*
> *In both the cases, pain is evolved,*
> *Be they unloved one or be loved.*
>
> [16/210]

> *Hence get not attached to anyone,*
> *As quite painful is separation.*
> *He who is not bonded to dear or not dear,*
> *Gets freed from fetters from either.*
>
> [16/211]

Grief arises from pleasure,
And from pleasure comes fear.
One who is free from pleasure,
Is free from grief and fear.

[16/212]

Grief arises from affection,
So arises fear from affection.
He who is free from affection here,
Need not worry from grief and fear.

[16/213]

Grief arises from attachment,
And so is fear from attachment.
He who is free from carnal pleasure,
He is then free from grief and fear.

[16/214]

Grief arises from carnal pleasure,
And from lustful desires arise fear.
He who is free from attachment here,
He need not worry from grief and fear.

[16/215]

Greed gives rise to grief,
And fear emanates from greed.
He who if free from greed,
Is free from fear and grief.

[16/216]

He who is always honest and upright,
He who possesses virtue and insight.
He who is faithful to his bounden duty,
Is dear to all for his truthful morality.

[16/217]

He who aims at blessed heights,
And who is not bound by carnal delights.
And whose mind is satisfied and steady,
He ascends the upstream of Eternity.

[16/218]

When a person is on journey sometimes,
And remains absent for a very long time.
Kith and kin, well-wishers show concern,
With great pomp and show, celebrate his return.

[16/219]

Similarly when a person leaves this earth,
And goes to the other world after death.
And if had performed good and virtuous action,
Like a returning relative, welcomed in heaven.

[16/220]

CHAPTER – 17

ANGER
(Kodhavagga)

Pride and anger are the most heinous enemies of a man. Anger develops greed and greed leads to quarrel. Only love can overpower anger and keep it at bay like wisdom eliminates lies and sacrifice eliminates greed. One should eschew anger and remain busy doing good deeds.

One should abandon pride and temper,
Keep body and mind under one's power.
When one has nothing, owns nothing,
He is absolved of all the sufferings.

[17/221]

Whoever throws the anger away,
Like not letting the chariot go astray.
He is then really called a charioteer,
Other simply hold rein at the rear.

[17/222]

Conquer anger by love and affection,
Conquer evil by noble action.
Conquer greed and avarice by generosity,
And win the liar by truth and sincerity.

[17/223]

Lose not temper and speak the truth,
Keep mind calm steady and smooth.
Give whatever little to the beggar,
Company of gods, these paths offer.

[17/224]

Those sages who control their body,
And do not hurt and harm anybody.
They are absolved of grief and pain,
Eternal Bliss they finally attain.

[17/225]

Those who remain agile and aware forever,
And train themselves nights and days together.
And Nirvana becomes sole aim to tend,
Their passions will soon come to an end.

[17/226]

O Atula, This is an old axiom on speech,
Blame a person who is reticent in speech.
Blame the person, too much who speaks,
Blame the person, moderately who speaks.

[17/227]

There was never one, and will not be,
There is none now, and nor will be.
There is none who is free of blame,
There is none, admired for fame.

[17/228]

Wise praise and advise a noble man,
Day-in and day-out, he is under scan.
Such a person is of flawless attitude,
Full of wisdom and model of rectitude.

[17/229]

Such a person can not be blamed,
Who is clean, pure and is not stained.
He is as refined as Jumbu River's gold,
Lord Brahma and gods shower praises unfold.

[17/230]

Guard against any physical misdeed,
Keep your body under control indeed.
Let go all wrongs of your body,
Practice strong virtue of your body.

[17/231]

Guard against any mental anger,
And control your mental temper.
Abandon all misconducts of mind,
Restrain and be calm all the time.

[17/232]

Guard against any verbal brawl,
And control your speech withal.
Abandon all verbal wrongdoing,
And lead a life of verbal well-being.

[17/233]

Wise who have mind restrained,
Have speech and body well-trained.
They are wise with senses controlled,
Need nothing else to keep under hold.

[17/234]

CHAPTER – 18

IMPURITY
(Malavagga)

It is very easy to find faults in others. A person should look into his inner-self and take a look at mountain of his faults and bad qualities. He should do penance so that he can make it easier to travel the path of death. Every one has to submit their account of life to God. It is better to settle such accounts before departing from this world by doing noble deeds, sacrifice and penance.

> *You are like a dried withered leaf now,*
> *Death is waiting to take you away anyhow.*
> *Eve of your final journey is almost handy,*
> *But no provisions for the trip are ready.*
>
> [18/235]

> *Make yourself a refuge, to live in,*
> *Make efforts to cleanse of your sin.*
> *You will then enter the realm of heaven,*
> *Provided all misdeeds you have forsaken.*
>
> [18/236]

> *Your life is coming to an end,*
> *The king of death is at hand.*
> *There is no rest-stop on the way,*
> *And no plans, you made for the way.*
>
> [18/237]

For yourself, make an island,
Before your death is at hand.
Be wise, cleanse of sins and guilt away,
To be exempted from birth and decay.

[18/238]

Let wise cleanse himself step-by-step,
And rid of his sin, stains and defects.
Like the silversmith, silver who does refine,
One by one remove impurities however fine.

[18/239]

Just as rust which develops on iron,
Eats into it without any reason.
So do the bad deeds and sins,
Lead the offender to his ruin.

[18/240]

Non-repetition is the blight of prayers,
The blight of house is lack of repairs.
The blight of beauty is laziness,
The blight of guard is carelessness.
(Blight-bane, damage, loss)

[18/241]

The blight of woman is misconduct,
The blight of a donor is mean conduct.
Wrong actions taint even the best,
Taints people in this birth and the next.

[18/242]

Ignorance is the supreme blight,
And can be called blight of blights.
O Monk! Get out of fetters of ignorance,
And rid free of this taint of ignorance.

[18/243]

Life is easy for one who is rude,
It is like a crow that is so lewd.
Who is backbiter and is arrogant,
Who is corrupt, uncouth and insolent.

[18/244]

But life is difficult for one who is modest,
And who is pure at heart and honest.
It is tough for one who has given up attachments,
And is now quiet, calm and intelligent.

[18/245]

A man who kills and destroy life of others,
And lies who always fear not to utter.
And unlawfully occupies other's asset,
In this world he digs his own roots at best.

[18/246]

Whoever takes, what is not lawfully his,
Drinks wine, goes to other's spouses.
In this world, he digs up his own roots here,
Pays for these evil acts in the world next there.

[18/247]

My man! Try to know the bad and evil,
What is difficult to control is only evil.
So let go greed and wrong-doing,
That drag one to chronic suffering.

[18/248]

People give offerings as per pleasure,
Keeping their faith as very dear.
Foodstuff given to others if brings envy,
Then day and night they do not feel easy.

[18/249]

But who is not discontented with offering,
And place full trust in their offering.
Envious feelings, who could dismiss,
Day and night, peace becomes his bliss.

[18/250]

There is no fire akin to lust,
There is no chain like disgust.
There is no net like delusion indeed,
There is no river like craving and greed.

[18/251]

Fault of others is easy to recognise,
But one's own fault is hard to espy.
One winnows other's fault like chaff,
But hides one's own by camouflage.

[18/252]

He who seeks fault in others,
And his criticism becomes severe.
His corruption continues to grow,
He is far from removing that flow.

[18/253]

Just as there is no path in the sky,
There is no saint to find outside.
While people enjoy mundane pleasure,
Awakened ones remain free from desire.

[18/254]

Just as there is no path in the sky,
There is no saint to find outside.
There is no creature who is eternal,
But minds of Buddhas remain tranquil.

[18/255]

CHAPTER - 19

RIGHTEOUSNESS
(Dhammatthavagga)

Lord Buddha deals with righteousness in this chapter. He advises that no decision should be taken in haste and nor should there be any partiality shown towards anyone. He further tells that a highly educated person need not be the most intelligent if he does not act in accordance with the scriptures and the rules. Similarly a clean-shave person is not necessarily a saint unless he has cleansed off his sins entirely.

The man who does not decide hastily,
But who investigates the matter justly.
And is impartial to decide wrong and right,
Is the man who is called just and upright.

[19/256]

Whosoever guides others by procedure,
Which is neither faulty nor unfair.
He is a guardian and trustee of rule,
Such a wise is impartial and lawful.

[19/257]

A person who indulges in effusive talk,
Is not willy-nilly wise and well-taught.
But one who is patient and without despise,
Friendly, fearless, free of anger, is wise.

[19/258]

A person who can profusely talk a lot,
Treads on Dhamma , necessarily he not.
Whosoever learns Dhamma in little talk,
And neglects not Dhamma, is well-taught.
(Dhamma-truth)

[19/259]

A person who has developed grey hair,
He is not necessarily considered an elder.
Ripe in age by years of life, may be that man,
He can not be elder but an 'old man in vain'.

[19/260]

An elder man has full control on self,
And has no desire for power and pelf.
He is a wise sage, truthful and venerable,
And is virtuous, faultless and a noble.

[19/261]

Man is not known by his mere beauty,
Or by eloquence which emanates envy.
He is not considered to be accomplished,
If he is deceitful, jealous and selfish.

[19/262]

But a person who does not harbor jealousy,
And who out and out believes in honesty.
But rather has gotten rid of deceit and greed,
That wise sage in called an elder indeed.

[19/263]

Shaven-head man is not certainly disciplined,
If towards sincerity and religion he is not aligned.
To call him a man of religion is utterly wrong,
Nor does he qualify to be called a holy Monk.

[19/264]

However, a person who is sincere and honest,
Untruthfulness and deceit who fully detest.
He can verily be called religious and a holy Monk,
For he has overcome evils with mind strong.

[19/265]

A person who just begs alms,
And adopts outwardly fake forms.
And if he partly adopts the Holy Scriptures,
He is not a Monk but a Monk imposter.

[19/266]

Only that person is qualified to be a holy Monk,
Who discriminates between right and wrong?
And who is not affected by honor or dishonor,
Sticks to scriptures is a Monk of the first order.

[19/267]

A person is not a sage by being reticent,
And especially if he is foolish and ignorant.
But one who prefers good values only,
That indeed make him a sage Holy.

[19/268]

One who has an eye to discriminate good over evil,
And who embraces good values and eschews evil.
He comprehends this world and the other,
He is called a sage who is wise and superior.

[19/269]

A person who injures living beings,
He is not noble and is damaging.
But one who does not hurt anyone,
Is indeed called a nobleman.

[19/270]

Neither by taking religious discipline,
Nor attainment by exercising meditation.
Or just by staying alone to remain in solitude,
None can achieve peace and beatitude.

[19/271]

However, bliss of renunciation I do relish,
Which ordinary people fail to accomplish.
O Monk, beyond mundane matter, I enjoy Bliss,
You also can enjoy peace, if sins you dismiss.

[19/272]

CHAPTER - 20

THE PATH
(Maggavagga)

This chapter tells about the path to truthfulness. A person who is endowed with this quality has the courage to face and fight the evils forcefully. It also cleanses the inner-self of a person and brings joy and peace.

Of paths, best is the eightfold,
Best of truths is the fourfold.
Virtuous person is detached and free,
He is the best if he has sharp eyes to see.

[20/273]

In this world, there is only one path,
Which helps purifying of inner-self fast.
Hence follow this path devotedly,
Which will confuse evil permanently.

[20/274]

Follow this path, confused evil will perish,
And so will, your sorrow and grief vanish.
Having learnt to remove the thorn of lust,
I preach this path as one of the best.

[20/275]

Awakened ones will show you the path,
But it is your duty to endeavour hard.
Meditative ones who practice this mode,
Are relieved of the attack of evil sword.

[20/276]

All created things are ephemeral,
All conditional things are mortal.
Whoever, this pure path befriends,
All his sufferings come to an end.

[20/277]

All created things are sorrowful,
All the processes here are painful.
Whoever, this pure path befriends,
All his sufferings come to an end.

[20/278]

All processes are not real,
Every Dhamma is without soul.
Whoever, this pure path befriends,
All his sufferings come to an end.

[20/279]

Though young and strong, fails to realise,
And rises not, when it is time to rise.
He is then weak, lost in sloth and insolence,
Never discerns wise path and its importance.

[20/280]

Watch your speech, control your mind,
Not to physically hurt, keep in mind.
Perfect these three courses of action,
As per wise, progress is then certain.

[20/281]

From meditation springs wisdom,
Lack of meditation is loss of wisdom.
Knowing these two paths of light and dark,
On the path of light, wise men walk.

[20/282]

Kill the forest of passion not just a tree,
Danger lurks in forest and not in the tree.
When you kill brushwood and the forest,
O Monk! You shall be free of lustful zest.

[20/283]

As long as the desire is not killed by man,
And carnality of man remains for woman.
His mind is fettered strongly somehow,
Like a suckling calf attached to cow.

[20/284]

With one stroke let go affection,
As if it was lotus in the autumn.
Cherish the path of peace and joy,
Nirvana shown by Buddha, you enjoy.

[20/285]

Fool thinks he shall live in rain and summer,
And that he shall live in autumn and winter.
He is unaware, what is in store in between,
Knows not the danger, death might intervene.

[20/286]

Man attached to children and livestock,
Is seized by death that carries him aloft.
Like the village ravaged, when in slumber,
By the fearful storm displaying its temper.

[20/287]

When the man is seized by death,
None can defend him on this earth.
Be it a son, father or a relation,
No body can offer him protection.

[20/288]

Wise is he, who ascertains these facts,
And emulates noble and virtuous acts.
Such a wise restrained by morality,
Clears the path leading to Eternity.

[20/289]

CHAPTER – 21

MISCELLANEOUS
(Pakinnakavagga)

It is well-known that sharing happiness does not destroy your happiness. Small happiness when shared with others, fetches large happiness. It is advised that man should follow the scriptures enumerated by Lord Buddha and try to get rid of all sensuality, greed, pride, false ego and anger. He should meditate in solitary forest to achieve *nirvana*.

If by giving up small pleasure,
One perceives enormous pleasure.
It is wise to let go small pleasure,
In favour of the larger pleasure.

[21/290]

Whoever causes pain to others,
To seek his own joy and pleasure.
He is then stuck in bonds of hate,
Which is very difficult to mitigate.

[21/291]

Neglecting what ought to be done,
And doing what ought not to be done.
Those who indulge in unmindful acts,
Their crimes continue to resurrect.

[21/292]

But in actions, those who are selective,
And do what is better and effective.
They are wise, alert, and mindful in act,
Their desires become fully defunct.

[21/293]

A Holy man may kill mother and father,
And may destroy two noble king-warriors.
Even if he destroys treasurer and subjects,
He is absolved of all grief of such acts.
(Mother-craving; father-conceit; two kings-
eternalism and nihilism; subject-sense object)

[21/294]

After having mother and father slain,
And killing two priestly king-Brahmins.
Holy man kills tiger, the fifth victim,
He goes his way; nothing perturbs him.
(Refer to note in verse 294 ; tiger-mental hindrance)

[21/295]

One who is the disciple of Gautama,
And practices recollection of Buddha.
In Dhamma remains ever awake,
Day and night, joy he partakes.

[21/296]

One who is the disciple of Gautama,
And practices recollection of Buddha.
In truth remains ever truthful,
Day and night, joys grow plentiful.

[21/297]

One who is the disciple of Gautama,
And practices recollection of Buddha.
In Sangha, he remains ever faithful,
Day and night, joy remains blissful.
(Sangha-community)

[21/298]

One who is the disciple of Gautama,
And practices recollection of Buddha.
And practice mindfulness of body,
Day and night, joy remains steady.

[21/299]

One who is the disciple of Gautama,
And practices recollection of Buddha.
And practices non-violence entirely,
Day and night, enjoys pleasure regularly.

[21/300]

One who is the disciple of Gautama,
And practices recollection of Buddha.
And delights in practice of meditation,
Day and night, he gathers delectation.

[21/301]

Hard is monk's life to enjoy this world,
Hard is to live in home to enjoy household.
Association with incompatibles is painful,
Avoid restlessness and path that is painful.

[21/302]

One who possesses wealth and repute,
And on path of virtues, remains resolute.
He is honoured and always respected,
Wherever he travels, he is trusted.

[21/303]

Noble men shine from far away,
Like the peak of the Himalaya.
Evil men are not noticed and decried,
Like an arrow shot in the dark night.

[21/304]

One who sits alone, and rests alone,
One who is resolute and acts alone.
And one who can control himself alone,
Joy derived in forest he does not mourn.

[21/305]

CHAPTER – 22

THE HELL
(Nirayavagga)

This chapter deals with the end result meted out to demoniac and Satan. Those ignorant fools, who perpetrate evil deeds, are lewd, wicked, greedy and indulge in carnality. They are all destined to go to hell. They are demoniac who do not believe in scriptures and are the greatest fools.

Whoever speaks not the truth, goes to hell,
Whoever backs out from act, goes to hell.
After death , both are equated at par,
To hell in the next birth, they depart.

[22/306]

Many persons who wear yellow dress,
Purity of mind they do not possess.
Such wrong-doers end up in hell,
In the next birth, in hell they dwell.

[22/307]

It is better for such unrestrained person,
To die by swallowing the red hot ball of iron.
Than to feed on alms offered by people,
And remain unscrupulous and immoral.

[22/308]

Four misfortunes befall the reckless man,
Who consorts with wife of another man.
Merits degrade, disturbed in slumber,
Debased to infamy, to hell he tumbles.

[22/309]

Debased from merit to evil destiny,
Meted out by Rulers, heavy penalty.
Both are frightened who commit adultery,
For short joy eschew the path of adultery.

[22/310]

Take precaution for trimming Kusha grass,
If wrongly handled, can chop hand fast.
Likewise life of a monk rings death-knell,
And finally drags him to abyss of hell.

[22/311]

When ill-performed are acts of devotion,
Performed with neglect, and vow broken.
And when holy life is not well-disciplined,
For any reward his life is not destined.

[22/312]

If act is to be done, do it right,
Do it with zeal and remain upright.
Purity, a careless man does not admire,
Besmears himself with mud of desire.

[22/313]

Ill-action is better left undone,
To avoid reprove from bad action.
But good deed if is better done,
His grief is then forever gone.

[22/314]

Guard yourself like a frontier fort,
Guard yourself well inside out.
Do not let go a right opportunity,
Otherwise hell will be the dismal destiny.

[22/315]

Those who feel awfully ashamed of,
What they ought not be ashamed of.
And ashamed of what they should be,
Go to hell as they uphold false view.

[22/316]

Those who fear what is not worth fearing,
But do not fear, what is worth fearing.
Such persons follow wrong path of discipline,
Which leads them to hell and oblivion.

[22/317]

Those who discern wrong, that is not wrong,
And see nothing wrong, what is really wrong.
Such people follow wrong path of discipline,
Which leads them to hell of perdition.

[22/318]

Those who perceive fault as fault,
And perceive no fault as no fault.
They are people of legitimate belief,
Blissful State they certainly achieve.

[22/319]

CHAPTER — 23

THE ELEPHANT
(Nagavagga)

Here Lord Buddha explains that a noble person is like a trained elephant who can weather all types of odds as an elephant is not deterred in war from the shower of arrows from all sides. When the noble person learns to control and conquer his sense objects, evils do not come close to him. He spends his time with learned lot like Yogis who enable him to come close to *nirvana*.

There are many who lack reticence,
I shall endure their painful utterance.
Like an elephant endures in combat,
Arrows from every corner it's shot at.

[23/320]

The King mounts on a tamed elephant,
One can take into crowd that elephant.
He who is disciplined is the best of men,
Endures criticism, serenity is not shaken.

[23/321]

Well-trained mules are excellent,
So are the royal-tusk battle-elephants.
So are thoroughbred noble 'Sindhu-horse',
Whoever tames oneself is best, of course.

[23/322]

Nobody can reach the untrodden land,
Even if he uses these animals, if he can.
But a tamed and self-controlled person,
Reaches nirvana without any obstruction.

[23/323]

Dhannapalaka elephant is hard to subdue,
When its temple runs with pungent juice.
When tied up, it refuses to eat foods,
Great tusker thinks of elephant of woods.
(Dhanapalaka is the name of an elephant)

[23/324]

If one becomes lazy and overeats,
The gluttonous then wallows in sleep.
Like a hog overfed on cereal grain,
That fool is born again and again.

[23/325]

This mind of mine used to wander,
At its own will and desire, it saunters.
But now I shall master and control somewhat,
Like mahaut controls the elephant in rut.
(Mahaut-the person who controls elephant)

[23/326]

Take delight in heedfulness of all kind,
Guard your thought, guard your mind.
Disengage yourself from bog of evil,
As elephant spins out of mud alluvial.

[23/327]

If you find an intelligent and wise person,
Walks with you, behaves like a companion.
Overcomes dangers, lives soberly and wisely,
Keep his company zealously and mindfully.

[23/328]

If you do not find an intelligent friend,
Who is nice, sober and willing to tend.
Then walk like an elephant in woods alone,
Like a king who renounces conquered throne.

[23/329]

It is always better to live alone,
As fool can never be a good companion.
Live alone with no evil and doing good,
Like an elephant roaming in the woods.

[23/330]

Good is friend, who always helps in need,
Good is contentment, what one has indeed.
Pleasant is to give up all grief and torment,
Pleasant is to have done good at life's end.

[23/331]

Good is filial devotion to mother,
Good is the devotion to father.
Good is to serve the holy men,
Good is to serve the noble men.

[23/332]

Good is virtue that lasts till life's end,
Good is faith which is firm and constant.
Good is acquisition of knowledge and wisdom,
And good is to eschew evil so loathsome.

[23/333]

CHAPTER – 24

THE CRAVING
(Tanhavagga)

Desires are the root cause of man's downfall. Desires once fostered, continue to grow and eventually become the cause of man's doom. They are like creepers which wrap around the tree and kill it. Even if one cuts down the tree, its roots are not destroyed, tree is again revived. Similarly if desires are not rooted out entirely, they come back and make inroads. Hence controlling the mind becomes very essential to keep desires away.

Cravings for heedless grow endlessly,
Like the creeper grows incessantly.
He then drifts from one life to another,
As monkey jumps from one tree to other.

[24/334]

Craving is like poison in this world,
Which overcomes a person, however bold.
His sorrows and grief continue to grow,
Like Birana grass after the rains, grows.

[24/335]

Difficult is to overcome wicked craving,
But whoever controls his selfish longing.
Stays away from his life, anguish and grief,
Like the water stays not on the lotus leaf.

[24/336]

I say good luck to all assembled here, of course,
Remove the root of Birana grass from its source.
Guard yourself from the evil's repeated sweep,
Like flooded river crushes the entire reed.

[24/337]

If tree is cut down but strong roots remain,
The felled tree will come to life once again.
Similarly dormant craving springs up again,
When roots of evil are not eradicated and slain.

[24/338]

Thirty-six pleasure streams, man does possess,
They can pull him to carnal lust and obsess.
And when thoughts are set on desires,
He is consumed by intense lust, like fire.

[24/339]

The streams are present everywhere,
And stays alive, the creeper of desire.
When creeper like desire begins to scud,
Be wise and nip the evil in the bud.

[24/340]

Sensual pleasure of being, is wide-ranging,
They are steeped with pleasure and craving.
Bound by happiness, they tend to seek again,
And undergo cycle of rebirth again and again.

[24/341]

Beset by lust, people run here and there,
And so besieged, run like terrified hare.
Sensual pleasure binds them in chains,
And they suffer in every life again and again.

                                    [24/342]

Beset by lust, people run here and there,
And so besieged, run like terrified hare.
Monks discard pleasures for sensual end,
And yearn for nrvana to continually ascend.

                                    [24/343]

Whoever is rid of forest of desires,
In solitude of forest, find pleasures.
But whoever runs back to household cage,
He, though free, runs back to bondage.

                                    [24/344]

It is human nature to hanker after desire,
Passion towards ornaments is like a fire.
Strong too is the desire for a wife and son,
Than to own just wood, rope and iron.

                                    [24/345]

Strong is attachment to these bonds,
Must remain away from these, holy Monk.
They degrade a person, are hard to rend asunder,
Wise Monk cuts ties and abandons all pleasures.

                                    [24/346]

Infatuated ones swirl back into tides,
Like the spider in its own web glides.
Monks cut off the sensual desire,
Vanish then, their sorrows entire.

[24/347]

Let go the present, past and the future,
Traverse to existence of farther shore.
When your mind is completely liberated,
From the cycle of rebirth, shall be liberated.

[24/348]

Whoever is tormented by evil thought,
And is dominated by the passion a lot.
He surrenders to the pursuit of pleasure,
And helps make the fetter stronger.

[24/349]

He who subdues his thoughts,
And meditates on the faults.
Who is ever mindful and careful,
He tears apart evil bonds so brimful.

[24/350]

Whoever has attained this goal,
Who is free of lust and is bold.
He breaks asunder the thorn of life,
Absolved of rebirth, it is his last life.

[24/351]

Whoever is without greed and cravings,
And understands the words and their meanings.
He knows the order and sequence of letters,
He is a sage absolved of rebirth hereafter.

[24/352]

Unattached, I am victor over all, I know all,
I am free of cravings, I have renounced all.
Since I have understood and realised fully,
Then whom shall I consider or call teacher really.

[24/353]

There is no gift better than truth,
There is no taste better than truth.
The joy of truth excels all other pleasures,
All grief evanesces with cessation of desires.

[24/354]

Riches and wealth can destroy the foolish,
Those who seek beyond, fool can't demolish.
But when wealth is craved by foolish,
He along with others tend to perish.

[24/355]

Fields are harmed by the weeds,
Mankind is harmed by lust indeed.
But what is given to those lust-free,
Offer and yield great fruits and glee.

[24/356]

Weeds are the blight for the fields,
Mankind is harmed by lust indeed.
What is given to those hatred-free,
Offer and yield great fruits and glee.

[24/357]

Weeds are the blight for the fields,
Mankind is harmed by lust indeed.
What is given to those delusion-free,
Offer and yield great fruits and glee.

[24/358]

Weeds are the blight for the fields,
Mankind is harmed by lust indeed.
What is given to those desire-free,
Offer and yield great fruits and glee.

[24/359]

CHAPTER – 25

THE BHIKSHU
(Bhikkhuvagga)

This chapter describes the duties of *Bhikshu* or *Bhikkhu* (monk). A *Bhikshu* has to learn to meditate in solitary place, learn all the religious scriptures and act upon them, keep control on all sense objects. He should be reticent in speech, eschew greed, desires, anger, false pride, etc. He should collect alms for food and respect it.

> *Good is restraint of the eyes,*
> *Control of the ears is nice.*
> *Restraint of nose is also cordial,*
> *And control of tongue is genial.*
>
> [25/360]

> *Good is control of body and of tongue,*
> *Good is control of mind and everything.*
> *Mendicant can control everything,*
> *And is absolved of all sufferings.*
>
> [25/361]

> *Whoever controls hands and the feet,*
> *And controls the head and the speech.*
> *He relishes inner joy with calm mind,*
> *Alone and contented, Monk in him you find.*
>
> [25/362]

Monk controls his tongue when teaches,
He is moderately reticent in speeches.
Unassuming, he explains teachings wisely,
Defines meaning in letter and spirit calmly.

[25/363]

The Monk who abides in the truth,
Delights and meditates in the truth.
Who follows and keeps truth in mind,
He never fades from the truth sublime.

[25/364]

Despise not offerings made by others,
Nor should you envy gains of others.
The Monk who envies other's gains,
Meditative silence he never attains.

[25/365]

Offerings made to Monk, however small,
Ought not be despised by the Monk at all.
Then, even gods will shower their praise,
If Monk is agile, is pure full of grace.

[25/366]

He who has no self-identification of any kind,
And has given up affection to body and mind.
He is called a true Monk who grieves not,
When he finds he has gotten naught.

[25/367]

The Monk who abides in Universal love,
And to the teaching of Buddha , is devout.
That Monk attains finally the Eternal Bliss,
Where existence ends, all grief dismiss.

[25/368]

O Monk! Empty this boat to make it light,
The sail will be swift, when it is light.
Cut off and forgo the hate and desire,
You shall attain nirvana — eternal pleasure.

[25/369]

Cut off the five and get rid of five,
O Monk! Master and develop the five.
When freed from the five bonds,
Crosses the flood, surely the Monk.
(1. Cut off five-self-illusion, doubts, wrongful rites and ceremonies,
carnal pleasure and hatred; 2. get rid of five-attachment to realm
of form, attachment to formless realms, conceit, restlessness and
ignorance; 3. Develop the five-confidence, watchfulness, effort,
concentration and wisdom.)

[25/370]

O Monk! Meditate, do not become heedless,
Let not your mind indulge in sensual happiness.
If heedless, you need to swallow the iron ball,
Lest painful burns will make you cry and yell.

[25/371]

There is no meditation without wisdom,
There is no wisdom who meditates seldom.
Whoever possesses wisdom, and meditates,
He attains nirvana, bliss of eternal state.

[25/372]

Monk who has retired to a lonely abode,
And who has eventually nirvana scored.
His mind is at peace, full of immense joy,
Supreme delight, more than human he enjoys.

[25/373]

When one is in a position to realise,
How the body elements fall and rise.
He experiences great joy and happiness,
Realising that nirvana is deathless.

[25/374]

For a wise monk it is important and necessary,
That he follows the monastic tenets religiously.
He must control his senses and contentment,
To be a holy monk, these qualities are important.

[25/375]

Let a monk associate with pure and noble men,
And who are resolute, possessing cordial acumen.
He should befriend who are refined in conduct,
He receives joy and suffering becomes defunct.

[25/376]

Look at the Jasmine creeper,
It sheds its withered flowers.
O Monk! You should take a lesson,
And give up hatred and passion.

[25/377]

Monk is calm in body, calm in tongue,
Calm in mind, that one is the Monk.
Detached to the pleasures mundane,
Serenity that Monk verily attains.

[25/378]

Lift up your self by yourself,
Scrutinise your self by yourself.
Monk who is self-guarded and mindful,
Will live a life of delight and joyful.

[25/379]

For self is the master of self,
And self is the refuge of self.
Self you must train and tame,
Like noble steeds, merchants tame.

[25/380]

Teachings of Buddha are guide to holy route,
Which offer immense delight and beatitude.
The Monk attains blissful state of peace,
Where conditioned things tend to cease.

[25/381]

He who follows the holy path when young,
As Buddha's teachings followed by Monk.
He illuminates the world with his clout,
Like the moon breaking away from cloud.

[25/382]

CHAPTER – 26

THE BRAHMIN
(Brahamavagga)

This last chapter deals with the requisites of a holy man (*Brahmin*). He should believe in *dharma* and respect the scriptures. He should follow these scriptures completely and teach others as well. He should remain aloof from mundane attachments like wealth, desires and believe in non-violence. He should be a person in whom people can place trust and his final aim has to be to attain *nirvana*.

O Brahmin! Cut the stream, go beyond,
Leave all desires and lust behind.
Knowing the doom of things created,
O Brahmin! Be a knower of uncreated.

[26/383]

In two states of insight and meditation,
When goes beyond duality, the Holy man.
When the Holy man knows the real truth,
All his fetters are broken from the root.

[26/384]

Neither this shore, nor other shore,
He who knows neither or both shores.
Free from anxiety and   unconventional,
He is a Brahmin, such holy person.

[26/385]

Free from fear and free from shackles,
Free from faults, meditative and settled.
Detached, accomplished and desireless,
Is Brahmin who achieves supreme happiness.

[26/386]

Sun shines by the day, and moon by night,
Shine in armoured shield , warriors of might.
Shines in meditation, Brahmin so bright,
Brilliantly Buddha shines in day and night.

[26/387]

Brahmin discards wrong and evil deeds,
That is why he is called Holy man indeed.
Hermit is one who lives in peace all time,
And who gives up faults is called pilgrim.

[26/388]

One should not hurt a Holy man with violence,
Nor should holy man hit back with vengeance.
Shame to the one who hurts a Brahmin,
Woe to Brahmin, if strikes back in retaliation.

[26/389]

Holy man does not gain anything,
If holds back his mind from dear things.
The sooner the intent to hurt vanishes,
The sooner all pain and sufferings perish.

[26/390]

Be it a body or be it a speech,
Be it mind, Brahmin restraints each.
He hurts not through three spheres,
I call him a Brahmin – the holy seer.

[26/391]

Whoever teaches the Dhamma doctrine,
Must be revered as a teacher of discipline.
Dhamma taught by Buddha we must admire,
Like the Brahmin reveres sacrificial fire.

[26/392]

Matted hairs do not qualify one to be Brahmin,
Neither by birth nor by family is one Brahmin.
He ought to be righteous and pure in mind,
He then passes as Brahmin; he will find.

[26/393]

Matted hair is of no use to Brahmin,
O fool! What use is your antelope-skin.
Inside , you are tangled in passion,
Outwardly you show clean emotion.

[26/394]

The man who wears clothes wornout,
And is gaunt whose veins stand out.
And one who is absorbed in meditation,
That is the man I verily call a Brahmin.

[26/395]

I do not call him a holy man,
Because of his mother and clan.
Who is supercilious owning wealth,
Who is attched, owns lot of wealth.

[26/396]

One who has cut off all fetters,
One who does not quiver and flutter.
One who is beyond any ties and bonds,
That is called Brahmin who is not bound.

[26/397]

One who has cut off both bond and strap,
Who has removed halter and the rope.
Who has removed fastenings and barrier,
That enlightened (Buddha); I call Brahmin.
(Strap-hatred; rope-heresay; fastenings-latest tendencies;
barrier-ignorance)

[26/398]

One who has not committed offence,
One whose real might is his patience.
Who endures reproach and infliction,
He is the man, whom I call a Brahmin.

[26/399]

Free from anger and free from lust,
Full of virtue and is totally devout.
And who is subdued, bears his final body,
I call him a Brahmin, the man so holy.

[26/400]

I call him a Brahmin — a holy man,
Who does not cling to sensual passion.
Like water stays not on lotus leaf,
Mustard seed stays not on needle's peak.

[26/401]

I call him a Brahmin — a holy man,
Who has relaised the end of pain.
Who has laid all the burdens aside,
Shed off grief, in nirvana he resides.

[26/402]

I call him a Brahmin — a holy monk,
Who discerns right from wrong.
Who is deep in wisdom and is wise,
To the zenith of nirvana he does rise.

[26/403]

I call him a Brahmin — indeed,
Who rarely has any needs.
Who is detached to household,
And wanders without an abode.

[26/404]

I call him a Brahmin — par excellence,
Who relinquishes all modes of violence.
Animate or inanimate, he kills neither,
Nor does he cause death to either.

[26/405]

I call him a Brahmin — indeed,
Amongst greedy, who has no greed.
Who is friendly amongst intolerant,
And who is at peace amongst violent.

[26/406]

I call him a Brahmin — a holy man,
Who lets go anger and aversion.
Who also lets vanity and hypocrisy fall off,
As from needle's tip mustard seed falls off.

[26/407]

I call him a Brahmin — a holy man,
Who imprecates and offends no man.
Who utters sweet and gentle speech,
Which has instructive and truthful reach.

[26/408]

I call him a Brahmin — holy above all,
Who takes nothing in this world at all.
That he is not given , be it long or short,
Large or small and good or bad of every sort.

[26/409]

I call him a Brahmin — a holy man,
Who has no desires and passion.
Who has no longings and lust,
Be in this world or in the next.

[26/410]

I call him a Brahmin – a holy man,
Who has no attachments and passion.
Who is free from doubts and is wise,
Nirvana, he is able to fully realise.

[26/411]

I call him a Brahmin – very holy,
Who is above fame and infamy.
Good or bad, indifferent he remains,
Who is pure without wants and pains.

[26/412]

I call him a Brahmin – a holy man,
Who is without any taint and stain.
He is pure, serene like the moon,
To desires who has become immune.

[26/413]

I call him a Brahmin – a holy man,
Who is beyond doubt and illusion.
Who has crossed over to other shore,
Calm, and meditative, but lust who abhors.

[26/414]

I call him a Brahmin – a holy man,
Who has no attachments and passion.
Who has ceded carnal desires and home,
Being homeless, wanders and roams.

[26/415]

I call him a Brahmin — a holy man,
Who has abandoned all passion.
Lives in solitude renouncing mundane life,
Desire for pleasure is not any more rife.

[26/416]

I call him a Brahmin — a holy man,
Who has given up bonds with human.
Delivered from all bondage and ties,
He then transcends celestial ties.

[26/417]

I call him a Brahmin — excellent,
Who is cool without defilement.
Who gives up anger and rapture,
Is hero, different worlds he does capture.

[26/418]

I call him a Brahmin — excellent,
Who is free from all attachments.
Who knows the death and rebirth of beings,
Who is blessed, awakened and free of clinging.

[26/419]

I call him a Brahmin — a pious and holy person,
Whose path is not known to any one.
Whose path is unknown to gods and spirits,
Whose desires are all gone and extinct.

[26/420]

I call him a Brahmin — excellent,
Whose is free from all attachments.
Who has nothing in his possession,
Be it before, after or in-between.

[26/421]

I call him a Brahmin — a great sage,
Who is noble and wise by any gauge.
Who is ever pure, steady in mind,
Free of faults, and is enlightened.

[26/422]

I call him a Brahmin — a great seer,
Who knows everything of life-earlier.
Sees hell and heaven, reaches end of birth,
Attains spiritual wisdom with no dearth.

[26/423]

THE END

BIBLIOGRAPHY

The following books have been consulted to prepare this book.

1. Dhammapada Sutra by Narda Thera
2. Dhammapada – by Thanissaro Bhikkhu (Geoffrey DeGraff)
3. Dhammapada by S. Beck
4. Dhammapada by Harischandra Kaviratna
5. Dhammapada by Acharya Buddharakkhita
6. Brough, John, Ed. The Gandhari Dharmapada (London: Oxford University Press, 1962). Dhammapada by John Richard
7. Carter, John Ross and Mahinda Palihawadana, trans. and ed. The Dhammapada (New York: Oxford University Press, 1987).
8. Norman, K.R., trans. The Word of the Doctrine (Oxford: The Pali Text Society, 1997).

Books on Hinduism

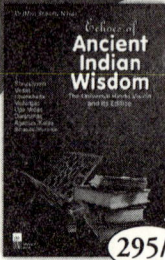

295/-
H.B.

295/-
H.B.

499/-
H.B.

399/-
H.B.

96/-

80/-

150/-

96/-

250/-
H.B.

140/-
H.B.

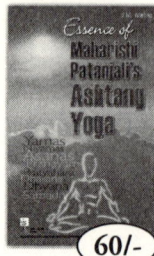

60/-

Books on Hinduism

195/-

195/-

499/-

H.B.

140/-

96/-

80/-

80/-

60/-

80/-

399/-

H.B.

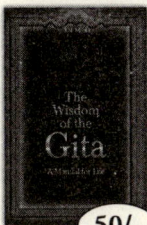

50/-

Postage:
Rs. 25/- each book.
Every sybsequent book:
Rs. 10/- extra